MW00446991

Author photo by

Florencia Vetcher

Published in the United States by

Fence Books
University at Albany, SL 320
1400 Washington Avenue
Albany, NY 12222
www.fenceportal.org

Book design by

Rebecca Wolff

Fence Books are distributed by

Consortium Book Sales and Distribution
www.cbsd.com

and printed in Canada by

The Prolific Group
www.prolific.ca

Library of Congress Cataloguing in Publication Data
       Reines, Ariana
       The Cow/ Ariana Reines

Library of Congress Control Number: 2011940190

ISBN 978-1-934200-56-8

SECOND EDITION

10 9 8 7 6 5 4 3 2

Portions of this book appeared, in slightly modified versions, in *The Ephemera Quarterly,*
Dear Bear, and *5_trope.*

THE COW

Ariana Reines

THE COW

CONTENTS

Sucking is dangerous. The danger of sucking.

The day is a fume. At starboard, a white kirtle which is the moon. The day has a hallmark, the night also.

Blue winter air. The chief leaf, which is a firm clasp on the smoke of days that keep on destroying my mind. It is not easy to be honest because it is impossible to be complete.

The end.

First there's wind. A single star like the pale hair of a girl. The dim universe plucked with light.

These were the bright muds. The light an asp rivets it. A sleeve of light. Beginning's navel. The nipple of the world. A crescendo. Meaning flies up, goes up, sails up before all fossils, before anything hard. Energy. What transpires in a crowd of eyes that are not yet. Wet eyes wet with energy which is sense.

No part of dark air lolls upon a single thing. Creatures like catamarans on tiny water. The faintest wing of air being cut by something existing. A radiance inside of time. A snail tracks the ooze that proves duration. Mammalian: beginning to be inside of her. Eventually time taking. This is writing.

He said, now I'm going to shit
Into your hand. Another voice appeared. You don't
Know me but I know you.
The emergency takes place.
It's a hole. Nobody knows how they got there.

Anyway I think it better to be a bassoon
Getting blown. This hand is my hand.
I could have been better but now it's too late.

Because of remembering where or what you ovum gasp and burst. First he spit on my asshole and then start in middle finger and then the cock slid in no sound come out, only gaping, grind hard into ground. Voluminous bounty of minutes sensate and glowing shoot out.

SHE say when she drink liquid it leak into her sinuses. HE grinding his stuff with his hand. SHE refusing operation. SHE want him to have murdered her. So he BROKE her eye she face brain. A day exist so I can not think.

Liquid shoot into her skull and leak out her eye hole.

Thick book like his fat head when I sit on it and fart. All signification room for all. Moistest mouth is cow's mouth sorrow face normal. Hung up hind legs reversed negated shit brains rear world.

Two prawns in the night.
Rakes, rakes. All wrapped in red. These are ways of budding at Little
Gidding. A hickory, a hind, undisturbèd lands.

Such soft songs were sung: having a nation.
Strands of the infomercial mommy and the recital is starting
Because we are American.

Lay deep in reverie, two troths into which he dumped me,
Forever, forever.
The sweet women are coming. Because we are American.

A quack made a cake.
A hickory, a hind, all wrapped in red,
Because we are American.

There is no order in this poem because it is mine own.
I hate the song.
So I can lie down and take it, take it.

Now I'm really good at sucking cock.
Lights in the herring, lights in the quivering river.
Lately I'm really good at sucking cock.

So quivers the river, so run the hinds.
We gather at the river. There is an order,
It is mine. We become the river's chump.

Having a nation is as good as having a language, Less possible, even,
Sculls on the water, than, less possible than the air that happens
Without your doing anything.

Eat me.
Eat me.
Silence of eternity.

Q: DOES A DAY THAT IS EMPTY DENUDE ANYTHING

A: It's dangerous to have feelings when you don't have any money.

Sunday has been inaugurated but the facts suffer.

A kink in the air because something is in it I am.

I held his cock while he peed with it.

A fond morning gets to know ourselves.

So the air sounds like a toaster buttressed with girls.

A kink in the air happens because the long-lost comes home again.

What happens when you look at something until nothing, until the world disappears.

Every line keens toward the same trough.

Every line leans over like heavy lilies, yes the simile, wanting to get dirty and die.

Sunday has been inaugurated and bells succeed the morning because inside them it gets dark.

We don't care what the fucker feels. Sensation that is something wholly other. Long night of the guts.

We are going to be smarter about these things from now on.

So many ways of being illuminated gas.

A gelid streak of apple goo a purl of it I peel away from me and eat.

I know that really beautiful women are never alone.

Their intelligence curls up like a fist in them and sweetens the shutter on their clits.

Even bodies have to exist in an environment.

Fleshy pink hood over those long lips.

Surviving. Aspics inside of which a day is held ajar.

When the difference between seeing and others, and all else, becomes clear as a veil.

I start to know something that is a membrane somebody licked onto my two eyes.

What a house begins as.

An assurance.

I can go on.

For someone to have done something with her own blood.

A house a skin can be. Was, it was.

The house could have been.

A declarative stance as personified by the house.

Is this shithole my membrane, do I have to feel the ends of what I feel by virtue of what it is.

Acres of wishes inside her. Any liver. To harden the gut. Boys rinse their arms in what falls from my carotid. My body is the opposite of my body when they hang me up by my hind legs. I mean the opposite thing. Not a wall with windows in it and flaglets of laundry waving or being so easy to mouth his so-thick. Sloes and divorcing her miserable eyes from the rumor they stir up in me. Everything on the planet is diverted.

Worse is less bloody pussies to lick. Everything good's an animal.

Asymptomatic. Causing one thing to fuck another. Introducing between one thing and another one of those copula which is an and. Genitals are for togetherness. Put her two feet in the stirrups.

I wish I could remember when it was her mouth fastened itself into the rictus of pure hunger she still wears. Her teeth the color of some kind of caviar or dirty marble, shining behind the waxen smear of mouth. I don't care what happens next except to see her. I don't want to know the end of the story.

So skyey guilty for existing. Light's a kind of bane. Fish fat. Factota. I need that man in my life.

In heat a lady could be other than what she had assimilated. Two breasts of almond paste. She smiled against the cracked varnish on her mouth. Pates basted in sunshine. Or whole instances of consciousness corralled inside themselves. What's the outermost border of a thought, what's the ordure of an event. In heat a lady. Tits swinging, white udders. Apertures. Woman make me. Want to be a jockstrap, shit-stained. Walled-in by her own substance. A car encased her or an agate. Steamships and pissoirs, the resinous accretion of pharmaceuticals in her. Antimacassars embroidered with zodiacs, gold threads, incisors, or womb. A little everyday renovation.

MY BELOVED PUT IN HIS HAND BY THE HOLE OF THE DOOR, AND MY BOWELS WERE MOVED FOR HIM

I look at the light it is a bug bleeding legs into the night. The light is here for somebody else.

We were cancellations shaken out of a bag. Something to be depended upon was there.

This writing is stupid. A mouth finds the moon in error and reverses its final poem again and again, for the last time.

Get over writing. How. **PUNCTURE ME SO I CAN RESEMBLE BEING ALIVE** Now. A gloss shimmers below what happens and acclaims it. The luster of something. I was part of they died. They are still fucking one room over. I think some sodden will means continuity. To become an ash-sieve, a bowel that processes things. A real institution.

Fuck it.

I walk into somebody else's house. I open all the drawers, cupboards. I look in the fridge. Medicine cabinet. Then I masturbate on all the pillows and bleed into the sink. I fix myself a drink.

Clean the language. Clean it.

I'm here to work GO GO so I can't call you. I'm here to work GO GO so I'm alone. When I'm alone I stink. I shit with the door open because there's nobody here and because there's nobody here I can taste my GO GO shit.

There's no malediction. No thought can poison me.

In the night you might as well not be in a country.

I feel like a sandbar sucking whiskey from a taser gun or brill cream. Finally your cock reimburses me.

"The best way is the hardest."

My sea of love. I want to tell you. My sea of love. I want to tell you.

Cannot have a "the world" but can have millions of guts through which the maize and antibiotics of "a world" are forced to pass.

I feel about you secondly, or secondarily, succeeding.

Succeeding is only going on. A second's not an instant it is simply not the first. All counting means not being at the origin.

"They call me the Meat Handler. Among other things."

I cannot count the altering that happens in the very large rooms that are the guts of her.

World translated. Words that could have been voles falling assfirst out her face.

glv ovr me. brns; ozne.
nckl sze POONANNY nthn anymre
Hre fr NEW YORK CITY

Cz nthn IS ITSELF BUT STILL BEARS
THE OLD NAME: EMPTIED VENERABLE
PU PU PLATTER. Rpeal ALONE mss.

FINGER THE DYKE TOWARD A GOOD
RECESS. convokd BEYOND lvng.
TOO MANY GULFS IN THE DAY MEAN HE BE

dyng. VETOING cz in secur. the stpd
STARS ARE blndspts. MORE HOLES. mre hls.
Crm up hs VISTULA. & WROTE DEAD GULL ON THE POOP

An alabaster fidget is impossible to imagine
Nevertheless they spent a long time wanting to fuck statues
And having hair that didn't move when a wave came.

The wave rises to a point and pierces the moon.
It is night. I have a jaw which could be a gunwale,
I have the night which is hemp cord in my hard hand.

Nobody fucking understands, when the building coughed up the white
Rubble of everything, whitening us with its dust, a little blood on our lips
We were the real's dead mimes. Or stained minutes.

This is a permanent poem. If I don't fuck today I'll die.
This is a poem the size of almost nothing: a blotter made rude
By its inexorable silkening.

A wobble ate canned pie filling and, like the centuries,
Grew into an angry augur.
All time is a piece of shit, nothing but a warning.

A hundred kneelers say the dark sky is rent with darker dews that shimmer like rot in the morning. This is the great divestment you heard about, a slow roan spreading over the hundred colors of the night

So suave, the night ending, a drawl upon the water, and everything goes together like a kit

It could be this easy to love you. It could be this easy for undestructed helpings of budding day to stack themselves up against an onslaught of light

And be everything, be as they are today, be as they might be tomorrow before the catastrophe comes. It could be this easy to have it all divide

You from it, so that somewhere somehow a you might dwell that could be more than conjecture falling in acid drops upon this ether of nothing, this cleanest of all possible airs

So what if I ate two bags of Lays. She doesn't give a shit for a word. It is not like making something in encaustic after all she said, to speak. She is happy like a shrub. The disinterested learners want to be happy. Have to become worse. Worse. She needs an emblem. I ate two bags of Lays and felt the cat cold over my heart, the brays of burros in the night.

The brays of burros in the night. I have to become everything.

Alone in here inside the universe. A catkin. She had wine-colored pants made of buttery leather. Her hair was rust-colored and her earrings were copper.

In the night I was going to be free. I was going to be lovelier and therefore somewhat more free. It was not going to be liberty anymore because the planet was closed. Now also the earthen parts of the planet are closed to you. Flowers are just pubes. You.

So moose and hounds were dead on the tar and softening and I knelt beside them in the wet tar and put my hands into their flesh with the maggots and the charades. The smell was oh and the sun.

I am just trying to find a way out of here. There were maps there were buttresses there were tools escarpments things I had to find out genitals glass-fronted IN CASE OF EMERGENCY a fool's will stranded on a pile of shoes. I am the execution and the life.

Papua Papua Papua Papua the world is real.
Papua Papua Papua Papua the world is real.

The experiments are finished already. Now for the tests.

We don't need you. Thank you for your interest. We adore you. Goodnight.

In the night I am going to be a blazon. There is going to be a taste in my mouth ordures.

I want to have an adventure. The restaurant is full of couples who met online. There are different sounds happening inside of the consciousness which is also changing. The rubber shoes. I want to be her.

I leave through her.
A tent made of midriffs. I am going to find out what love is.

I asked him what he did. He was lying on the floor with two coats on him. He said, first I got some scissors and I cut part of her wig off. Then I tore off her wig. Then I punched her a few times in the skull. Then I threw her on the floor. She got up and I threw her on the floor again. When I hit her in the face finally she said something. She said, Oh my god, I think you've broken my nose. Then I got a screwdriver.

A roof's invaginated ornaments, the lowing of the dark cattle under a stand of air.

I then you pluck the procession out according to the text that prescribed it.

We know it must be better than what we can say for it.

We know our intelligence will betray the clits of sorrow that shudder and jerk off the last of day.

We don't care. We don't care. We don't care.

A bolus of words passing from one world into the next, sourer and sourer, worse and worse, aloner. Mooted,

Rent, rubbered, hated, ended, ended

Anyway the solid girl was not going to hold water.
So puncturing her didn't matter in the end.
She wanted me I wanted her beveled under the eaves.
I did not want to follow her she did not want to follow me.
She was not less than I. I was under the eaves.
Culture throats full of the files of days and books are the same as nets
For time shit, sieves that catch an air's leavings.

How much hate I hate.
How much hate I hate.
A mass of slow.
A slow cancel.
How much I hate.
How much I hate.
A realism.
I account for myself by virtue of a process
Because some other energy drives me.
How much I hate.
A realism.
I can animate the virtual. I can be.
I can animate the virtual. I can be.
A slit of difference, a vent in the real, a realism.
How much hate I hate.
An air possesses the older food.
An air possesses the feed.
The sun! Somebody is still alive, inside of the air. An air possesses the
Old.
An air possesses or encompasses the intensity.
There is no lens on the air.
Sharded of coal, sharded of sebum and hair,
Sharded of motes in a past that is dead but will not go.
How much hate I hate.
How much hate I hate.
How much hate I hate.

I am a mart in the dog and look, here's some merchandise. I am a mart in the dog. Aye.

Being a mart in a dog is like being a world: overstated.

Do you know what love is if you are a mart in a dog. You sell Hoodsies and cigarettes and lotto tickets. You are real.

Do you know what a dog is if you are trapped inside of him.

Everything is part of something.

I am part of something because my life is so stupid.

Being a mousse made of stars in the night that I want to feel is being too because I am gluey like a girl.

I even am a girl. Wow, fuck me.

Being a night inside of the mouth of a loved boy. Red black and shiny teeth with a tongue. The word of a loved boy has sense.

In a mart where there are newspapers and burnt coffee all the night long, bic pens in a jar, scratch tickets and pornography, everything's ok. I am not the nice man in the mart I am the mart itself, which is inside of a dog who would love me by instinct except he doesn't know I am inside of him and a mart isn't an I.

Infinity has got to become mine so that I can know which way to turn, so that I can know in what direction something like morning is breaking.

There was a kink in the thing that was a girl
It wasn't enough
There was a mutt in the girl but it wasn't enough
It wasn't enough ENOUGH ENOUGH for what
It wasn't enough FOR ANYTHING TO BECOME TRUE ENOUGH
TO LIVE ON EVEN THE TINIEST LITTLE BIT
There was a stool on the girl but nothing happened
There was a loom in the light
There was a loom in the light but nothing was allowed to come of it
Because it wasn't sweet it was
SOMETHING BURROWING THROUGH THE DAY
Another day came
It became a sore ONLY
POETRY STARTS TO KNOW WHAT A DAY IS
I was not among the things it was
There was no room for me
Others were there
They were enough.
I was a sock filled with rubble
CROTCH
I was the shaft some light filled
I was a skin
They filled me with something
I was a LUNG
There wasn't enough for her to go around
There wasn't enough of her
She was a DISH
A LATE HAND

EVERYTHING UNDER THE SKY IS POSSIBLE
JOY
She felt like everything inside
Once you got inside something started to happen
I was a rock PLUGGED
I was a hole EMPTIED
I carried myself I wended my way I caused my own footfalls
I was a device
I caused my existence CROTCH
Nothing has got necessarily to do with anything else
There was a horn in the girl A RAMPART
It was too complicated
BRANDING
To be named.
To be altered.
To exist.
I could try to get to know you.
Find out who you really are.
Apprise myself of what you are.
Keep abreast of yer
GLAMOUR
MY BRAINS COULD BE USEFUL IF I DIDN'T FORCE THEM TO FEEL
A carcass is a widgeon big enough for one.
The beauty of the ocean.
The lovely weather we've been having.
Because there is no music, the words might unfurl from their mouths like
A scroll.
A skiff IS a corpse.
Your face was like milk poured into the sea. You spilled your drink on the
Ground and took your shirt off to clean the ground. I licked you. I licked
Your low back JOHNNY. I licked my way up your back bowed low.
It was a night. There have already been enough nights.
I have loved you forever. There will never be enough. I was bleeding

When we finally fucked I forgot. Being a person. Walking away.

You smell.

I could become a hole for time to pass through me

Or eat me.

Wrap me in sailcloth, make me a paper, a reflective thing. Entrust me
With loaded days, prime me like an ether, charge me with a salve or
Unfinished minutes, fuck me so I can keep on disappearing.

THE MASSED AIR

Weighs on me like a pillow.

A pillow of salt. Nothing can hide me.

Have me.

Overnight they grew purple with blood. In the morning nothing was left.

COULD THERE BE A NIPPLE IN THE DAY.

Something to flow out of.

A knowing that could make us. That could save us.

A way of feeling.

A form. A formula. A feeling.

The very ends of light are to hold you fast.

I hate the beautiful air. Slow shadows scrawling their way.

A drawl hangs upon the air.

Something you get OVER.

Something that in time you get over.

To be a chit wiving the wind.

To wash. To wash away.

A gloss shimmers below what happens and speaks also. Grave flickers my
Delight. Cedars, cowls, ampoules, all of you put a fist in the applesauce.
You crush water, lop the halves, pining for them limpid and clear, and Yet.
The event bleeds into time before it gets there.

He locked you in the bathroom and peeled off your rubber pants and
Fucked you on the sink so hard it broke away from the wall. The end.

To speak tears an asshole into the air. You couldn't come. It's a slot for
Your thinking, the rigid wavelength of your voice leaving me, leaving
Me.

A finer puce is another way to hurtle a wattle of the real. Or you could
TRY to be a vintner of it, and cultivate it, and care for it. If it decides
It needs you. Wants you. Except you're the stain on everything, or the
Thing between the dike and the water, delaying the disaster is what your
Body's for MY GREAT HEALTH
The air is not unless you circulate it.
Boils with fish. I bury my hand in your apple-dark. Language ripples
Outward. Your quickened palm. I am as dark as you when I close my
Eyes to breathe. I shoot liquid.

We can put the book between us and see each other by virtue of it. But
Still not know what of our hide our wants beveled.

A slut for you.

Liber, live, leaf, liberty, libra, leave, liver.

Even the melon weeps. And it is enough for us. And I am redeemed. A
broken vessel in a pot of parts that work me. A pot of parts that break me
and work me and break.
The place where a bobolink nods is worse than the blank gash in you
That doesn't even recognize you and doesn't care but eats your emeralds
Anyway because if they stank of your incursion they could begin to signify.
They could begin to die. And then you'd never be alone again.
But to ram it up and constantly is not a repair.
Let's pretend it's night. Let's pretend we're about to begin.
The spittle of righteousness, the north, the law, vigilance agog, we are
Clanging against the forge, unparcelling that of which we have been
Made.
Because martial knowing has taken away from the cell its humility.
Tend Water. Formulate if honey could be intelligent, Put to use even the
widowed Instant of a shadow causing the twinge of your knowing ending,
Because without us, WITHOUT USE WHAT IS A THOUGHT

She is only ever the exact shape of her thought because it obliterates the Ground upon which it keens when falling into flower in her. HE THREW A TUNGSTEN LAMP AT HER AND IT BROKE AGAINST HER BUT THEY LOVE EACH OTHER. If they love each other, for whom is it to define, or Defy their love. LET THEM BE like provisos we could always undue IF The time comes.

A cow is not sacred. A cow is taboo. It is not that you have to worship her. You just have to not kill her. If you are Hindu.

In Sanskrit, transliterated, she is called AGHANYA, that which may not be slaughtered. She is also called GO.

A cow is a name for a heavy woman or a woman with sloe eyes. Cow is a common epithet for a slow woman or clumsy woman; a woman with a foul smell. A thick-lipped woman, an unintelligent woman, a woman whose features possess a disturbing combination of ugliness and sensuality. A woman whose desire to fuck exceeds the desire of others to fuck her. Also: to have a cow.

One who is ridiculous. Inherently ridiculous, irrespective of context. An impassive onlooker. Or: What do you call the meat around a cunt. Often: a witness. Silent.

A cow is a ruminant; she grazes and ambles, she stands still. Is flatulent, lazy, patient. She is named a ruminant not only because her relaxed and melancholy demeanor lend to her a philosophical—if gourmandizing— aspect, but because of the uniqueness of her digestive system.

The four compartments of her stomach are the rumen, the reticulum, the omasum, and the abomasum. The rumen, the largest compartment, contains billions of bacteria, protozoa, molds, and yeasts. It is because of these microorganisms that the cow is able to digest large amounts of grass. The bacteria and protozoa inside of the rumen digest what the cow eats. They produce volatile fatty acids and supply most of the energy on which the cow lives. These microorganisms also produce protein and nitrogen, and vitamins B and C. The reticulum has a honeycomb-like lining and functions as a trap for foreign objects the cow might ingest unwittingly, for example, rocks, or nails, or pieces of wire.

The omasum is also called "the book" owing to its many leaf-like folds. It is the gateway to the abomasum and aids in the reabsorption of water and fatty acids, though its complete function is unknown.

The abomasum is also called the "true stomach" as its function resembles that of the human stomach, producing acid and some enzymes.

It is worth noting that the cow's digestive system has been a mystery and a wonder for many centuries. Courses in animal husbandry and "agricultural best practices'" continue to make use, for demonstration purposes, of a live cow into whose side a porthole has been opened, and onto which opening a window has been fitted, so that the curious student can observe—with his or her own eyes—at least one stage of the animal's magnificent digestion.

The mouth of a healthy cow produces between twenty and thirty-five gallons of saliva each day. Some sources say fifty. This is to moisten her food, which is grass. The cow does not eat protein, she makes it. Her stomach turns grass into her body. As in, meat, which is good to eat. One thinks of a cow living on grass, that is, one imagines the cow living, literally, upon it, but a cow does not, not so much, not in the United States. In the United States, after she has been alive about six months, and if she is not one of the luxury "grass-fed" varietals, the cow lives in a stall on a feedlot, in Kansas, for example, like William Burroughs. She has got to shit where she eats, in the stall. In the stall she is fed FEED. FEED has many things in it, for example, corn, lots of corn, and, until recently, but maybe still, rendered animal. Rendered animal, for extra protein. Also, antibiotics. The antibiotics make it possible for the cow to digest the corn, which, without antibiotics, would kill her, but which, with antibiotics, makes her fat, which is to say, TENDER. Marbled. HEALTH.

Cud is a bolus of partially-chewed grass that she regurgitates or belches. The technical term for this is eructation. When she eructates, carbon dioxide and methane come out of her mouth along with the cud. She can't really make cud out of corn. The cud is kind of everything. A poem should not be merely topical maybe. But a topic can be poetical. Where is the text inside of her. Meaning is not a symptom, not only a symptom. A cow doesn't have to be a girl. A cow can be a bull. A steer is what used to be called a bullock, which is to say a bull that has no balls.

The woman was alarming in her hive of salt not talking along the flank of the first cooling carcass or a flood of insects upon a melon steaming, being the right kind of death, having ever been plump at all. A glove of minutes in the sac where usurers store their secrets of how they knew the keenness of a warning.

Here is what happens when a cow is slaughtered. She has shit caked on her, she is led down a gently-curved ramp; hundreds, thousands of cows are led down such ramps every day. If the slaughterhouse is a state-of-the-art facility, designed according to the innovative parameters of the world authority on abattoir architecture, Dr. Temple Grandin, then the ramps will be curved in such a way that each animal can see two animals ahead, and not more, as they wait in line to be stunned, bled, and processed. The Knocker is first: The Knocker administers a stun: a stun is a metal bolt shot into the brain, so that she won't feel any pain. This cannot be done in Halal and Kosher facilities, whose strictures demand that an animal be conscious at its demise. After the Knocker knocks her, she is hung up by her hind legs and her throat is sliced open. She is bled on a moving conveyor belt. Everything happens very quickly. An animal is costly. Industry has an aesthetic. They cut the head off and slice the carcass in half. If there is shit on the outside of the animal, this is shit's chance to make contact with the inside of the animal. Therefore, disease. Disease is not the only derivative of her.

I think there is a loom of glosses somewhere, where their weaver weaves them into a tissue that signifies and is real, that contains its own explications.

A wimple fell over the real as if to protect it: a ruckus in the girl is artificial as anything, fortified with nutrients. The corridor where centuries meet, the reverse nipple like a dimple in time. Depression into which certain irreplaceable musks collect. They are from elsewhere. Also: an autumn evening is a corridor.

I used to live in an apartment in Washington Heights where five other people also lived, and then my mother, because she had no place else to go. The people who lived in the apartment were not my friends. It was the cheapest place I could find. I found it through Columbia University, where I had been a student. That's all. Earl, the owner, liked to read old copies of the New Left Review while sitting on the toilet, with the door open, smoking a pipe. Earl had gone to Columbia in the seventies. Edna, who did most of the cleaning in the apartment, had covered the walls and surfaces of her bedroom with black-and-white Holstein cow paper, the kind of paper that is adhesive on one side, contact paper. Edna was a deacon at her church and had lived in the neighborhood ten years or so. Before that she was in jail for twenty-five years because she killed the man who raped her. Edna and Earl were black and Earl had an education and Edna didn't. As long as everything's copacetic, Earl kept on saying to me, then we'll be fine. Why don't you shut the fucking bathroom door I said.

I'm claustrophobic, he said. Maybe this sounds like bullshit but it's true, even though I know that truth is no justification for the poem. I never asked Edna what it was about cows. Sweet Edna. There is a huge market for tchotchkes of the cow persuasion. Who is into this stuff. Women. Unfucked, solitary women. Many many websites are wholly dedicated to the sale of such goods as cow bunny slippers, cow tableware and underthings, cow telephones, cow clocks. The signifier of the cow is much more popular than, for example, the signifier of the bull, despite the Spanish, the Minoans, Georges Bataille, Picasso, etc, at least in terms of the production of cheap goods. Edna was a nice person though something of a hypochondriac and she lived in mortal terror of Earl, or at least she said she did. Earl, once or twice a week, would lock himself in his room with a jug of Smirnoff and blast The Rolling Stones, Edith Piaf, and Public Enemy on his stereo. And sometimes he would holler, Ahhh Ahhh Ahhh. He smelled like garlic and fat and the alcohol made all the odors stronger. He listened to Edith Piaf especially, over and over. During these binges he did not leave his room and would piss and shit in a corner. When he got through the liquor he would order Chinese delivery. He probably still does. Edna cleaned up after him, even the excrement. Maybe he charged her lower rent. She bleached the floors and sprayed the toilet with harsh disinfectants many times a day. The walls were full of holes, and insects of stupendous variety would bask around the electrical sockets and faucets and drains. It was shortly after this period that I learned of my mother's interest in Creutzfeldt-Jakob, the brain-wasting disease associated with Bovine Spongiform Encephalopathy that fills the brain with holes.

A dish of farfalle the humping world. I am speaking I am just telling. A word that doesn't escape. Estranged. A poem is in the world therefore it is of the world. A symptom. Uh. "At any rate, what a vapid idea, the book as image of the world."

An umlaut, a diphthong. A zone in which kinds of matter are translated.

Silt and shit could have to do with each other. As fertilizer. Learning how to be a slit in the flailing palindrome this day is, this hockey puck of a book, too dense to make a room for me in it, no object but to be batted about the slick ice. Likewise a cow could be a way to be. Women: They can't get over their bodies.

Mad cow disease was discovered in the United States for the first time in a Holstein cow that was too sick to walk but was nonetheless slaughtered and sold for meat. The mad Holstein's brain and spinal column were sent to a rendering plant somewhere, possibly to be turned into dog or chicken food; possibly to have its blood rendered before being fed to young calves as a milk supplement.

One day my mother and I met by the river, presumably to have lunch but neither of us had any money. She was rolling her cigarettes out of Midnight Special Menthol and smoking them with the kind of black plastic holder you don't see in New York except in the ghetto. Her russet hair was hidden under a wig, also russet. Burnt umber. Orange. She looked thin but swollen because she had walked all the way downtown from Washington Heights to meet me in order to save the two dollars. Her lipstick was waxy and cracked and her beautiful freckles and dry hands with their spots and veins. Teeth like raw shrimp. Chest blotchy and sunburnt, soft, and Alfred Sung perfume. Red feet, platform shoes. I need a steak she said. I just feel so sluggish. I need the iron, I need the protein. What about Mad Cow I said. Well, yes, she said. How do you get it anyway, I said. Prions, she said. My mother was trained at Bryn Mawr, Jefferson Medical College, and Sloan-Kettering and she used to practice medicine. Prions are abnormally-formed proteins and they are extremely resilient, she said. And even though hundreds of thousands of heads of cattle have been slaughtered and incinerated, there are cow derivatives in absolutely everything. In lipstick, in plastic. Everything. And there is no way to know. I want a steak. So I gave her six or seven dollars and she went to Western Beef. Trying to feel like the put-upon daughter whose fault nothing is and trying to feel cool. This was when the Meatpacking District still had meatpackers in it, and sometimes still, whores. Not long after the nightclub MOTHER closed, not long after the restaurant PASTIS opened, not long before the designer stores moved in. Now what do you want to do, I said when she came back to the corner where I was waiting, smoking a Dunhill. I had given her pretty much all the cash I had on me. We could go to Chinatown and look at all the dried fish, she said, licking her cigarette paper.

No body means you are finally free. Illbient is a word to name something that is music. Bent is a way to describe you, who are. That the order of things, as soon as it is uncovered, should begin to budge.

I don't know a worm from a turd, but I know what the weather feels like. There is not enough sensitivity in the world. There are too many things to explain.

A pearl of sound, a pearl that doesn't mind not to be an emerald or an onyx or a sore.

That's how to exist. To be a blank upon which the hells project their sorrow and to forgive them, that means to be a mother. I love to write. My whole body writes.

My whole body writes.

I am the bride of my baby, I am the bride of this ok day. The sun is a peeled yolk. I broke.

I = Miss Havisham. Combustion heaven. To be changed, to go up up up, to be translated. HOW DO THE BEASTS GROAN! THE HERDS OF CATTLE ARE PERPLEXED, BECAUSE THEY HAVE NO PASTURE, YEA, THE FLOCKS OF SHEEP ARE MADE DESOLATE

I hate you and therefore we will be together forever, slice me open if I ever smooth this over, slice me open if I ever soften, if I ever moisten, if I ever fall for you again

He hollowed out a part inside of himself for nothing to be there.

It took effort.

Finches grommeted the wall.

I allowed so much seeing to murder me.

Below what I know.

She's a tube that shoots the poison in because she is a woman with warmth and I am losing it.

Fucking the cool girls, mouths that reverse themselves automatically.

I think I want a waltz to pretend to be me for a while.

Okay booboos staking the lone claim and they aren't enough to live on like a wraith.

It isn't enough, any of it.

It isn't enough to live on.

I am wearing your lacerated face. The eructations of bare air are visible on me. Nothing goes on in time for free. Dear lady, dear lady, the sun is wooly today and I am its forlorn human. All wordedness withstands something which is just about having a face. Or maybe only wordedness withstands it. Not under-stands but with-stands. A bad music flagellates the air. When is your skin not dressed in air. When you are swaddled, when you are buried. What is going to happen to the women. Could you fasten them down for me. I was going to escape being one. What pelts the identity of a thing, my heart, worse than its coquettish way of seeming to be there? I'm dead.

DEAR AUTHOR

I can't feel. What world is it you write inside of. Who happens to your way of writing and makes it become real. Who harangued you to make a sense that would belong to your name, or what. Willing a body to come out of the word worries the old magics but you have to. Don't you have to.

DEAR WOMEN

I know that you are not cattle. I feel alone inside of you. I walk around and the dead insects go crunch crunch. I don't know what to say about your beauty. What is it exactly about the feeling of excludedness a certain kind of girl makes you feel in your arousal. Dear complete women, dear intelligent women, dear women who do not take things lying down.

Wonder where the game is more like tinder in a tackle box. Find out where the future holds. Body is whole, body hurts. Body is whole, body hurts.

The girls get it together. They get it together, it works out for them, whatever. We were all from concentrate. Do not make meaning be so cute. No possible mother. Firmer, all pore, everything hounded. Holey face the idea pours out of face. Buttes, lumps, putti made of scar tissue which are gonna be faces. So in the concentration deep in the concentration all the rubbery body means gets bulldozed in the movie.

Nobody cares about your intelligence I do not care. I want a world to live in. I want a world to live in and I am vomiting cause there is no world. There are vessels that have had their innards emptied out, sliding around in the lube. Boinking her potato face with his thick stuff and she put a disease on his meat so it oozes green.

Glove my idea in an ethic of seeing. Cocked the butt high up it was my butt he put his thumb in LOVE. The writing rains down on the world. What if we all bent against a page? Not because we knew who we were but because we want the world?

Tender hand making a place where a world could get birthed. Plants allowed to sleep at night the dog lopes around a hedgerow and a purple feather also in the blue and green faucet out of which the night pours because the plants are allowed to sleep, and the pillow supports her cheek and a dream is allowed to be inside of the zone of her allowed to be alive because the love lies thick on her.

Time's up for mommas time's up for mommas they're all gonna get too old for longer and longer and die slower and slower and you're not gonna care, are you, gentle reader. By then the roaches'll cover the water and I'll live in a jute house and bathe in piss and become a real artist. She say call yo motha she suckled you she carried you a burning glyph inside the vessel shat you out you were supposed to turn out to be a spaniel. Nothing else happens in the nothing. We become like herring in a net. We become like people who don't know how to say anything. Like whatever I draped myself in the night, the orange streetlights and a Tartar vest that belonged to somebody, quit your fucking job, quit your fucking job and a chickpea salad soaking into the paper plate, Carla knows more about hedge funds and is futural, Booty is like die die die.

Imagine a dark for the writing to go around. The dark can be a place. The gut. Imagine it. The mental city means it's built of menial jobs that make it become itself. The mind. Uncensored thirties. A hovel to live in. The best way to go is the endlessest. I will not train myself to love this shit.

It is nothing to have a ruined face
Or something to keep in a flask and observe
It trembling.
Nothing. No. Not at all   .
The pure hard word
Stiffening on air
A column of notes refuses all minutes
A bead burrowing
Down along the heald

If a note could have wintering
As voices from another room gasping
Keep aloft the feeling of their ending
If a note could have wintering
Hardening
The keenness at the end of a curl
Incising the impossible air
A bled
Night its chilled glass
With a moon in it
Voices from another room

As a sieve of weighing and redress and a kind
Of mule
And they're at it harder and harder
Ramming a little bit
Of everything
It is nothing

To have a ruined face
Because with it

You can still crouch over berries or
A stand of black grass
If there were any deeper to go, some tambourine
Or other
The dusk would be
Or dulcet things
A moth suggests in filthy light
A flimmer upon ruination that is general
CORAZON
My dirty hub

Don't go
Assizes wormy or vast controls
And girders in the night
Environmentally sound
Having the white underthings and jiggy
Nodules and instants widowed
Or perfect in their singularity
Is how it is
As clear as I can be

She clasped the event to her and proceeded. Fucked her steaming eyehole and ended it. The cracked thing was a doomed pidgin, it meant something

Yesterday. A patience would be ideal. Make an art of it, sere notes winding their way through an air to have become the name of her going. Her name on the list, and some certain information they had.

After a time there is no more accuracy, after a time you can't get the note clean of what it might have been.

Under the skirt of Mother Ginger huddle little boys and girls. A holiday shit stain. His scholarliness justifies those flights

Of fancy you condemn in him. And the gummy hulls of words muzzle the chaw, a kind of cud that will not do. An umlaut could be a cousin's bone,

The poisoned nuance that started everything. It was from eating ourselves. It had to be

Someone else's sickness first, our silence, our good balance, our usefulness. There is something certain creatures long for. To be hacked up and macerated. That's having it come out and go into another body.

Eaten, gemmed with grease and herbs. Whose low language ruined our bowels. Whose lowing eventually meant nothing. We knew we were to become a ream of flesh. Another nothing.

Two sylphs trying to climb down off a note
Are nothing for the mystery of their exteriority.
Moo goo gai pan equals the sunset and slowly
But surely my girl's brain is the universe.
This is the best chic drek of the puppy day,
The final feeling of slow learners rounding a bend.

This is the best of two wombs competing for one hot stay.
It's the wobble her expiration looks like, which
Is a booboo ruining the tragedy she prepared for it.
He wants to be more culpable than me.
We wear the war, shoot the piano, bleach her panties.
A sun slavers over hairs and woofers
And the lady's cracks cleave to her nightie and just as hipster bitches get tanked,
Ruin their makeup and fuck sobbing and bareassed on the sidewalk
Bleeding bad air and sorrel, slashing their perfect tits, getting carded,
The usual taxation, no fun, self-confidence, worse than nerd boners etc,
And no hand comes to pierce the perfect night.

It was strong feelings in a Lollard
Sacristy. Or not. But so-and-so
"Loved history" as much as I adore to hear
The radiator hiss like a corridor
Full of fakirs silently padding.
You want to embrace the gunnysacks,
The brass buttons and mutton chops,
The sackbut, the horsehair, the mumps. You
Feel you must be a scroll of Victorian
Linoleum that never got put down,
Are sure a chronicle of occurrences must have to do with time.
What can I say? I feel a tenderness for the hare
Fretting over frozen lumps in some painting
I saw once. The face of the Virgin has been gouged
Out, so that she is blue cloth falling in regular pleats
From a confused knot, a kind of sacred necktie
Floating in a yolk of gold. She is all that's left, and must
Answer for me and the familiar travails
Of a distant foghorn, which is certainly the lowing of a dying lyric
Poet in an age that isn't ours, all that lipstick, all that tempera
Suckling at chalk. A constellating dew--
And arrant shit heads scrawling the usual
GO GO
I love you I love you I love you

Maybe there is still something on the night that smells of pleasure or maybe I am the dead one. Winch not fattening or getting, but browbeaten and curtailed enough times to be meaning something in how curtailed I am. It's not possible to fabricate a whole book out of memory. It's making, synthesis, or something worse. I am benighting the flowerbeds. Asphodels and beatnuts, I am having them. I am having my way with them. Having a coke with you. Being around. Gulls and diggers for pantoums, a wisp of fishers and breakers, a night in which to cure.

Maybe the night still has something in it that stinks engorged like sentiments. We took the night out to rinse it in owl loins weary and sugared, the afternoon with its normal trees and everything. All me have a little bit of you in them.

So it's better not to digest according to whim, underthings, according to what little can be gotten out of the knot in the wood. Need a method. Get a method.

"I haven't the heft to make care / Come out of jungle bagatelles or out / Of such humid Andean scurf. Neither / Heft nor its attendant comforts and sureties; / The niceties of southern order—oranges / And guitars, sea glass slowly boiled / And speared with toothpicks in a dish. / A shingled shed, wrung dog gaunt / As weathervanes, raven fins of hair, / The pale scrivener's afternoon / Of macaroons, of cormorants and pears. / Wait and want is all, said one type / Of haunchy mother, whether or not / You haunt gessoed halls or rub / The huffy nightingales that flit about / Haughtier kinds of doom. A letter / Falls open on the desk. The plume / Trembles in its tusk. In the gutter, / A bacon rasher and some weeds. /

You woke up this morning. / A sheaf of black birds rising through white /
Sky. Slimly, a wraithish hug. Sun up: / The nimming hay-van, burnished
rooves"

I am tradition. Go all the way. It's time.

I don't even remember what sex I think you were but I blew you.

This is where the night has to have its leash, where the gooseflesh rides
home to its owner, where things get arraigned and tightened and firmed
up in the crotch of violent light. This is where the night loses its power.
The lamps trained on leaves, leaves slick with light, the heavyweight
drama you want to have here.

I am not shivering because of the pain. I am shivering. It is that there is
something inside me, with which this writing has to do. Oh crap.

The smooth cheek of her.
Things were getting clear.

As long as it's not to be another carceral jenny, how your mind always
seems about to open and everything, as long as it's not another night
alone with the bottle,
                              whiffs off her panties. What happened in
America? Putty the shape of the whole that needs plugging.

The root and core of things, rotgut wiving how everything loved seems
shit pellets discharged with prestige and accuracy across that inevitably
female seascape.

As though a fistula were something you were really walking around with,
when it was just the gout of wanting breaking

In order to have the blessed morphology, to prepare for Plantagenets their wickers and blessings, a Moor dim ebonies.

The faded sound of a dandy fooling on a wasted farthing turning down my face for sorrowing redness your love's what I blame on your mother. Then the air becomes sticky, and I am too sorry to know how I feel.

I rake the dumpster across rubble because all I ever wanted from you was a goodnight kiss. Said the clitty bonehulls addled by dogs WE FEEL NOTHING WE FEEL NOTHING deep down in the tatters of the idea

Copulate Jakartas and nosebleeds having their fun with me for Benjamin Britten's mastiff sang as well as that. Never heredity worried me more, wilting sovereigns staining my tweeds, and I still know better than to ice the dagger before humping it, flipping the hard nut out of my buttonhole and the dead of pidgins and kneesocks set aflame in famous cunt. But I should be able to be better than that maw, performing whither and thither among the briars whose tides are normal woolenclad boys. This is my sacrifice, I put a gluegun up my thing and plunge the plunger because I want to die secreting hardcore dimities and lace strands dried in her chancre-shell. Herd me here into the glorious ever and ever above. For you are ever and ever amended my child. Ever and ever amen.

Time is somewhere else.

Don't they call a body the wound with nine holes. Why cannot a body itself be testimony. Why cannot the fact that the witness *is* bear the witness. Testimony's gesture of veracity used to be the laying of a hand upon the genitals. Why cannot being itself bear anything without a proof. FLESH MADE WORD

Constant presence of everything BE MY FRIEND longing.

You have got to goad yourself toward a becoming that is in accordance with what you are innate. You have got to sometimes become the medicine you want to take. You have got to, you have absolutely got to put your face into the gash and sniff, and lick. You have got to learn to get sick. You have got to reestablish the integrity of your emotions so that their violence can become a health and so that you can keep on becoming. There is no sacrifice. You have got to want to live. You have got to force yourself to want to.

And when Musa said to his people: Surely Allah commands you that You
Should sacrifice a cow; they said: Do you ridicule us? He said: I seek the
Protection of Allah from being one of the ignorant.

I'll let the night dissolve in runny shit.
I don't even mind crushing these bugs into my skin.
I can let it all stiffen into lines.

The great writer's grammar of resignation
Can do nothing to me anymore, because outside the wind is roaring.
And I don't have to worry about that either. I don't have to.

There's no law. And my term
Is almost ended. I have been expiring inside it as much as possible
And as long. I feel I'm on a balcony now, overlooking it all.

Now that my face is become a hood
Over the pulp of bad stuff that daily harms its outlook. Now that I know
That it is not for them I cry but for me. For me.

How come she has got to die before I can really have her.

Cuz in heat she used to become other than what she had assimilated.

Delve into the marzipan of her rutted teats.

You have got to squeeze her squeeze her squeeze her.

VALVE

I was stupid enough to put my mouth on his round mouth. Every O is if not a Messiah then seems a future. Mwa. Tongue cut my heart out because it does worse than love, it talks.

VALVE

My Warsawa got so hot. He wasn't going even to try to love me. Oh pooches, need me! Up her ass a maggot smelling of leather and amber and hair, Baudelaire. What does a country need a poet for. To put bunting up on the dead shanks of dreams.

VALVE

His thick thick thick in my Warsawa. So basically you peel the skin off and slice the thing in half with a chainsaw, vertically. Does every man really want to split me open.

VALVE

My Warsawa lost her way drownded in the River Bug. Harpists with hair long strands of brown fish shit. Downloaded today's sugar and the thick one wants to know if I'm coming over only if this muscle can forcefeel.

VALVE

Spackles the info bits. Language is the kind of failure inside of which you learn to fall in love. Much of her giant digestion has to do with metaphor or is it, is its essence. I don't care about my sorrow anymore because I and the minors who used to be me are not curable. Giantessa, hide me.

VALVE

Hide

VALVE

WR2 (Waste Reduction 2) PROVIDES UNIQUE INTEGRATED SOLUTIONS THAT ARE ENVIRONMENTALLY RESPONSIBLE, FOR NON-INCINERATION BASED DECONTAMINATION, BIO-CONTAINMENT AND DISPOSAL OF MEDICAL, BIOLOGIC (ANIMAL CARCASS) AND LIQUID EFFLUENT WASTES.

EU APPROVED

THE WR2 TISSUE DIGESTOR SYSTEM EFFECTIVELY AND RELIABLY ADDRESSES INFECTIOUS ANIMAL CARCASSES AND INACTIVATES PRIONS. THIS TECHNOLOGY IS USED SUCCESSFULLY WORLDWIDE.

To address a carcass is to liquefy it. This is real poetry. The tissue digestors come in all sizes. "Cadaver" sized digestors are perfect for humans or animals of similar size.

THE 7000 POUND CAPACITY DIGESTOR FEATURES
* FULLY AUTOMATED SIEMENS TOUCH SCREEN CONTROLLER WITH OFF-SITE DIAGNOSTICS CAPABILITY MONITORED BY WR2 ENGINEERS.
* IDEAL FOR ALL ANIMALS INCLUDING LARGE HORSES, COWS, MOST ZOO ANIMALS, PATHOLOGIC WASTE, AND ANATOMIC WASTE.
* IDEAL FOR VETERINARY SCHOOLS, LARGE PHARMACEUTICAL COMPANIES, LARGE RESEARCH CENTERS, UNIVERSITY AND MEDICAL SCHOOL FACILITIES, COLLEGES OF AGRICULTURE, AND GOVERNMENT AGENCIES.

This is real poetry because it's a vat of signification. What is made to pass through. It's language, it looks and sounds like language. Dissolve me.

GENUINE ALTERNATIVE TO INCINERATION

A NON-BURN TECHNOLOGY THAT REPEATEDLY ACHIEVES GUARANTEED STERILIZATION OF TISSUE WITH A FULLY AUTOMATED SIEMENS PLC THAT INCORPORATES REMOTE DIAGNOSTICS AND ARCHIVE CAPABILITY. THE WR2 TISSUE DIGESTION PROCESS IS NO LONGER JUST AN ALTERNATIVE TO INCINERATION; IT IS THE INDUSTRY STANDARD FOR ENVIRONMENTAL SAFETY!

If you can find out where meaning begins can try to follow it down to where it might end. Siemens was a major consumer of concentration camp labor during that war but in 1998 they lost a lawsuit and subsequently established a reparations fund to pay their ex-slaves. Environmental safety! they ejaculate. A machine that digests the planet's great digestors. Whose illness eats their brains because they were forced to eat one another. Who are become a risky aliment. Signification is antique and staid. Fuck me. Excising symptoms that are corpses from the world. Maybe I already have what she's having. How come this is not allowed to be exterior to the poem. Because the poem does not shoot out from a source it is of the world. While American poetry dissolved its I the starvational and massacred bodies of all the world larded newspapers with their blood

and guts. Shit. LYRIC. An integrity must come back to a body, and from thence, into a world, a world where a body can adore another one, or the sun, or a part of a thought under it, or the night. Maybe nobody wants to kill you because of what they think you are, or rape you, or treat you like a piece of shit. Maybe you don't need an I. An I's a dress literature can wear to be everything. Want to be infinity. Speaking but over yourself. Can a book carry you into the world you have to pretend doesn't exist most of the time, can a book carry you back out into what first made you alive. Muscles in their marbling enfolding the sickest livers and the saddest eyes, and tongues that flop out pinking as they desiccate. The secret of their ruminations and how easy it is to please them. WOMEN, WHAT DO THEY KNOW. THEY HATE THEIR BODIES. In the Song of Songs it is written that

she is only one of her mother

A NICE PERSON

she is only one of her mother

DO MY PART

she is only one of her mother

ACCEPT THE THINGS I CANNOT CHANGE

she is only one of her mother

POETRY DOESN'T NEED ME BUT I NEED IT *NEED* IT BECAUSE I FEEL SO FUCKING LAME

the Song of Songs that is Solomon's says "she is only one of her mother"

SOUTINE SAW IT WHEN HE PAINTED CARCASSES OPEN LIKE RAW CUNTS

Sometimes I think cities are just bowls or catch basins that exist to always be tipping their contents into a trough and that's how come when I walk around in them I feel my body being emptied of all meaning

SOUTINE HAD A FACE LIKE A RAW CUNT SO HE MUST REALLY

HAVE KNOWN

What is exhumed not from the earth but from a body itself is an addictive kind of beauty you can't easily get over, and the decadent smell in the Peter Luger dumpster in summer and in Soutine's studio with its flies and rays and sides of beef didn't make women want to fuck him any less

INDUSTRY IS EVERYTHING

Sometimes I think if I can find a way to really feel my mere going could become as succor to the ruined women I love but it never does. The guilt of knowing the world's evil and still wanting to live in it

JUST SAW OPEN AND SEE

That which the palmerworm hath left hath the locust eaten; and that which the locust hath left hath the cankerworm eaten; and that which the cankerworm hath left hath the caterpillar eaten

END

Where are the men I have seen them. Where are the men. Where are the men. Where are the men they space out like dodgems. Where are the men. Where are the men. They suck stuff out of carburetors, they go to war. Where are the men. They are perfecting their craft. They are holding down jobs. They are learning to hate themselves just like us. Where are they. They are on suicide watch or where are they, they like to fuck but not to kiss, where are they. Where are the men. Where are the men. Where are the men I fucked them they are on pills. Where are the men. Where are the men I fucked them. Where are the men I fucked them. I fucked them. and they don't know where they are. Where are they.

Black milk, black cocaine, brown piss, pink kisses, men. Men.

Do you then believe in a part of the Book and disbelieve in the other?

(Koran)

I have to get to the other side of the animal

LIVESTOCK MORTALITY IS A TREMENDOUS SOURCE OF ORGANIC MATTER. A TYPICAL FRESH CARCASS CONTAINS APPROXIMATELY 32% DRY MATTER, OF WHICH 52% IS PROTEIN, 41% IS FAT, AND 6% IS ASH. RENDERING OFFERS SEVERAL BENEFITS TO FOOD ANIMAL AND POULTRY PRODUCTION OPERATIONS, INCLUDING PROVIDING A SOURCE OF PROTEIN FOR USE IN ANIMAL FEED, AND PROVIDING A HYGIENIC MEANS OF DISPOSING OF FALLEN AND CONDEMNED ANIMALS. THE END PRODUCTS OF RENDERING HAVE ECONOMIC VALUE AND CAN BE STORED FOR LONG PERIODS OF TIME. USING PROPER PROCESSING CONDITIONS, FINAL PRODUCTS WILL BE FREE OF PATHOGENIC BACTERIA AND UNPLEASANT ODORS.

Across her. Across her.
Upending the weight of her I have to be finding out a grammar.
How to be. Opener.
Sawed open. Easy.
Open like a grammar.
A dust of light the air carries.
What is a night upended.
A carcass in which nothing is leftover.
What is a night upended.
Open, a hole where the head disgorges its body.

RENDERING OF ANIMAL MORTALITIES INVOLVES CONVERSION OF CARCASSES INTO THREE END PRODUCTS—NAMELY, CARCASS MEAL (PROTEINACEOUS SOLIDS), MELTED FAT OR TALLOW, AND WATER—USING MECHANICAL PROCESSES (E.G. GRINDING, MIXING, PRESSING, DECANTING, AND SEPARATING), THERMAL PROCESSES (E.G. COOKING, EVAPORATING, AND DRYING), AND SOMETIMES CHEMICAL PROCESSES (E.G. SOLVENT EXTRACTION). THE MAIN CARCASS RENDERING PROCESSES INCLUDE SIZE REDUCTION FOLLOWED BY COOKING AND SEPARATION OF FAT, WATER, AND PROTEIN MATERIALS USING TECHNIQUES SUCH AS SCREENING, PRESSING, SEQUENTIAL CENTRIFUGATION, SOLVENT EXTRACTION, AND DRYING. RESULTING CARCASS MEAL CAN SOMETIMES BE USED AS AN ANIMAL FEED INGREDIENT. IF PROHIBITED FOR ANIMAL FEED USE, OR IF PRODUCED FROM KERATIN MATERIALS OF CARCASSES SUCH AS HOOVES AND HORNS, THE PRODUCT WILL BE CLASSIFIED AS INEDIBLE AND CAN BE USED AS A FERTILIZER. TALLOW CAN BE USED IN LIVESTOCK FEED, PRODUCTION OF FATTY ACIDS, OR CAN BE MANUFACTURED INTO SOAPS.

Can you carry.
Allopathy.
I don't know. Harried. Aloofer
Like that fact of the sky.
Still we say things to each other inside of holes.

CRUSHER: MACHINE CONTAINING BLADES OR KNIVES THAT
GRIND RAW MATERIAL TO UNIFORM SIZE

A dirndl under the light is making me be.
Something far away.
Like becoming the weather.
Militating, she goes.
The facts suffer.
Eating her na nas. I don't want her but I have her.

PERCOLATING PAN: A TANK WITH A PERFORATED SCREEN THROUGH WHICH THE LIQUID FAT DRAINS FREELY AND SEPARATES FROM THE TANKAGE

Vented into the forge an analogy.
It blew in there because it thought.
It resembled. A sample of influence.
Using a world to build thought out of.
It is a poem of how to be.
Nobody is preceding too much.
And the form, the form,
An implement of several trains
Of thought. Is it worse to say
Otherwise.
Ow my body.

GRAX: SUSPENDED SOLID PROTEINS

Extruded.
Northerly, harmony of difference
Omigod more semen. Religion has a golden sound.
And a medium shoots out of the need.

CRACKLINGS: SOLID PROTEIN MATERIAL DISCHARGED FROM SCREW PRESS OF RENDERING PROCESS AFTER REMOVAL OF LIQUID FAT

I don't care. My gut is sour. Leaning into the bowl of air under him.

STICK LIQUID OR STICK WATER: THE VISCOUS LIQUID LEFT IN
THE RENDERING TANK AFTER COOKING PROCESS

Because remembering could be loose like interpersonal relations. I am
only a citizen. Nothing is required of me. Certain things. Maybe speaking.
This doesn't have to be speaking. Under speaking. Low. Down. Under
speaking.

TANKAGE: COOKED MATERIAL REMAINING AFTER THE LIQUID FAT IS DRAINED AND SEPARATED

Habile dews in the memory of all thinking are the sharpened. Things of the world. You have armpits too. Awaiting, clemently, clemently awaiting what comes of remembering.

Z VALUE: THE TEMPERATURE INCREASE REQUIRED TO REDUCE THE THERMAL DEATH TIME BY A FACTOR OF 10 (OR A ONE-LOG CYCLE)

A serpenting is recollecting and can happen. The feeling it is going on forever like an animal with a mouth. I am detachable from the work. Not true. Preexisting facts constitute the climate into which the work shoots.

TALLOW: THE WHITE NEARLY TASTELESS SOLID RENDERED FAT OF CATTLE AND SHEEP WHICH IS USED CHIEFLY IN SOAP, CANDLES, AND LUBRICANTS

Alimenting the world perpetuates it. Duh. Plus "the world" is itself a food. We go outside we stay in. I am going to try to be a girl. Try to transcribe bare sustenance. Reprimand some light on a brass latchkey. So many rents in the air.

THE EMERGENCE OF BSE (bovine spongiform encephalopathy) HAS BEEN LARGELY ATTRIBUTED TO CATTLE BEING FED FORMULATIONS THAT CONTAINED PRION-INFECTED MBM (meat and bone meal). AS DORMONT (2002) EXPLAINED, TSE (transmissible spongiform encephalopathy) AGENTS (ALSO CALLED PRIONS) ARE GENERALLY REGARDED AS BEING RESPONSIBLE FOR VARIOUS FATAL NEURODEGENERATIVE DISEASES, INCLUDING CREUTZFELDT-JAKOB DISEASE IN HUMANS AND BSE IN CATTLE. ACCORDING TO UKDEFRA (2000) (United Kingdom Department for Environment, Food and Rural Affairs), EPIDEMIOLOGICAL WORK CARRIED OUT IN 1988 REVEALED THAT COMPOUNDS OF ANIMAL FEEDS CONTAINING INFECTIVE MBM WERE THE PRIMARY MECHANISM BY WHICH BSE WAS SPREAD THROUGHOUT THE UK. THUS THE RENDERING INDUSTRY PLAYED A CENTRAL ROLE IN THE BSE STORY. EXPERTS SUBSEQUENTLY CONCLUDED THAT CHANGES TO RENDERING PROCESSES IN THE EARLY 1980S MIGHT HAVE LED TO THE EMERGENCE OF THE DISEASE.

Concentrate. The sorrow is humiliated.

EDIBLE TALLOW: EXCLUSIVELY BEEF, THIS PRODUCT IS RENDERED FROM FAT TRIMMINGS AND BONES TAKEN FROM FURTHER PROCESSING AT A SLAUGHTERHOUSE. BECAUSE OF THE ASSOCIATED PROCESSING AND THE LIMITS OF RAW MATERIAL, THE PRODUCT OF LIGHT COLOR AND LOW MOISTURE, INSOLUBLES, UNSAPONIFIABLES, AND FREE FATTY ACIDS, THE TALLOW MAY BE FURTHER REFINED, POLISHED, AND DEODORIZED TO BECOME A COOKING FAT. THE PET FOOD INDUSTRY GENERALLY USES THE CRUDE PRODUCT NOT SHIPPED UNDER SEAL. THIS IS OFTEN REFERRED TO AS TECHNICAL TALLOW.

A grain of brain. The day's bowels emptied out into the window white light. I was no one and I was not going to be. They let me out today but I have to go back tomorrow and I will. I don't want them to hurt me more than I already know how to handle

HASHER: A CHOPPER OF MATERIALS (A FRENCH WORD)

Well there's that cloud.
The mountain's goiter.
You shoot off into a broth of thought.

ALL EMITTED ODORS SHOULD BE TREATED IN CONDENSING UNITS FOLLOWED BY OTHER CHEMICAL SCRUBBERS OR INCINERATORS (AFTERBURNERS) AND/OR BIOFILTERS FOR NON-CONDENSABLE ODORS

Even if you don't believe it, the event, a bug in agar, is stranded somewhere inside of the real, being itself. How streetlights become cockroaches, aglow and bleeding into the filthy glue of night.

DOWNER COW: THE TERM IS FREQUENTLY APPLIED TO A MATURE DAIRY COW THAT IS STILL RECUMBENT 3 HR AFTER CALVING DESPITE TREATMENT FOR HYPOCALCEMIA. A SECOND TYPE OF INVOLUNTARY STERNAL RECUMBENCY IS ENCOUNTERED LESS COMMONLY IN CATTLE OF ANY AGE UNDER CONDITIONS NOT ASSOCIATED WITH PARTURITION AND FOR WHICH THE MOST LIKELY ETIOLOGY IS TRAUMA. DOWNER COWS THAT ARE ABLE TO ACTIVELY CRAWL ARE OFTEN REFERRED TO AS "CREEPERS" AND ARE CONSIDERED TO HAVE A MORE FAVORABLE PROGN- OSIS THAN INACTIVE ANIMALS. THE CAUSE OF THE RECUMBENCY IS, MORE OFTEN THAN NOT, ELUSIVE EVEN TO AN EXPERIENCED CLINICIAN. FURTHERMORE, INEXPERIENCED CLINICIANS MAY MISS AN OBVIOUS CAUSE IF THEY DO NOT ADOPT A SYSTEMATIC APPROACH TO DIAGNOSIS.

You learn to subtract yourself from it. And a night happens, like the night that goes on inside your organs, cause it is so dark in there, a night that knows you and how you are, and how it is going to be, a night that is packed down like a hard brick of hash or an opium made of the underside of everything that has ever glittered, which you can feel, which you know, which you carry with you because it's you, the dukes you are not going to put up to the real, the way you are going to keep on knowing what you know and going as you go, and how you will never totally disrobe it, how it will never turn completely to smoke, how it will never intoxicate you enough and how your substrates are never enough either, but you and this interiority will go on, on, for a while.

It's downers who have to be dragged to the knocker cause they can't even walk down the ramp. They get mashed up or transubstantiated and used to get fed to the ones living in their own shit at feedlots and that's how come thousands more had to be slaughtered and beyond slaughtered destroyed because DESTROY IS BEYOND SLAUGHTER incinerated or liquefied in special vats. The container contains the corpse. Something gets out from under the end.

VAGINAL EXPLORATION IS MANDATORY IN EVERY PERIPARTUM, RECUMBENT COW AND MAY LEAD TO DISCOVERY OF A DECOMPOSING SECOND FETUS. DAMAGE TO AND INFECTION OF THE WALL OF THE VAGINA IS COMMON. METRITIS AND AN ASSOCIATED TOXEMIA CAN CONTRIBUTE TO POSTPARTUM RECUMBENCY.

What happens to the world when a body is a bag of stuff you can empty out of it.
Errors, musculatures.
Can I empty language out of me.
What difference does it make how a thing dies. Consciousness. Nobody knows what that is.

RECTAL EXPLORATION IS ESSENTIAL FOR DIFFERENTIAL DIAGNOSIS. THE DEGREE OF UTERINE INVOLUTION SHOULD BE APPROPRIATE TO THE NUMBER OF DAYS POSTPARTUM. BALLOTTEMENT OF FLUID IN THE ORGAN OR LACK OF TONICITY SHOULD BE NOTED. UNEXPECTED ANOMALIES MAY BE PALPATED. ADHESIONS, LUMPS OF NECROTIC FAT, AND ENLARGEMENT OR TURGIDITY OF THE CERVIX OR VAGINAL WALL ARE ALL SEQUELAE OF A DIFFICULT BIRTH. FRACTURE OF THE PELVIS MAY BE PALPATED PER RECTUM, PARTICULARLY IF AN ASSISTANT MANIPULATES THE LIMB. TRAUMATIC INJURIES TO THE PELVIS OCCUR AS THE RESULT OF AN ANIMAL SLIPPING ON CONCRETE OR ICY SURFACES. THIS CAN OCCUR WHEN COWS RIDE ONE ANOTHER DURING ESTRUS. MOVEMENT OF THE HEAD OF THE FEMUR IN THE OBDURATOR FORAMEN MAY ALSO BE DETECTED. UPWARD DISLOCATION OF THE HIP OR FRACTURE OF THE FEMORAL NECK CAN BE CONFIRMED IF THE AFFECTED LIMB APPEARS SHORTER THAN THE CONTRALATERAL LIMB. TO CONFIRM THAT THE CONTRALATERAL LIMB IS NOT INJURED, ROLLING THE COW OVER TO EXPOSE THE LIMB ON WHICH SHE HAS BEEN LYING SHOULD BE DONE TO ACCOMMODATE A REPEAT EXAMINATION. PELVIC FRACTURES CAN BE ASSOCIATED WITH SCIATIC NERVE PARALYSIS, WHILE UPWARD HIP DISLOCATION MAY BE ASSOCIATED WITH SOME DEGREE OF OBDURATOR PARALYSIS. IF EITHER CONDITION IS SUSPECTED, THE SENSORY STATE OF THE LIMBS SHOULD BE EVALUATED. INVOLUNTARY STERNAL RECUMBENCY MAY BE ASSOCIATED WITH VERTEBRAL LYMPHOSARCOMA, ABSCESSES, OR BIZARRE TRAUMATIC INJURIES.

An animal secretes a lot of cortisol if you harass her too much in killing her and this ruins the meat you are trying to turn her into.

If her flesh can be ruined because of how marauded she feels can the air be ruined if she cries out inside it.

Who if I cried out CREAM O LAND

Who if I cried out

Who if I cried would hear me etc.

What happens to air that has rubbed up against mistrals, miasmas, or worser, nameless winds.

What happens to an air that carries the screams of what is under slaughter.

When she howls it's with her mouth.

When she howls it's with her mouth a tooth missing in it.

Menthol cigarettes and mozzarella cheese, coffee and sour apples.

Ma Ma. MOUTH MOUTH

Mean ME ME everything I can feel inside

What skin. What hair. What eyes, gold tooth. What muscles. What udder. What are hooves. The liver, what liver. What stomach. Horns. Where isn't she. Where isn't she inside her body. Where is she not. Where is she least.

There was a whole body that went before me: it was her.

Stretch marks on her stomacher.

If you want to know what living is do not ask a doctor.

Where am I not in my body, where am I least in it. What could be excised from me most easily.

Where is a living thing not itself. Is her shit any less her.

And moreover, gender.

It is latent in her until it comes out and then it can belong to her.

Because I am too solid I am an apparatus attached to the question.

Where does life exist. What if everything could be as tender and durable as a genital.

I want to found a country where everybody feels.

Universes shooting out of matter so tiny you can only feel it.

How to be liquid how to be gas how to be Freon, music, how to be flesh or inside of flesh that is living and how to be its equal, how not to be less than it, how not to divide the capital from the provinces, how to be.

I know this is not a poem because it is sputum. Also a curtain of veilleities hides stars. It's an environmental day. The spasm fills, never fills, the blood completely, and at this point a wooden bell tolls too, tofu on kitchen tile, the sound of polite existence, some taxis in the romance, since it's raining, and doubt muzzled in a disposable diaper every day all day. The man said there was maggots in there, there was everything. Mimes. Mimes in meat dresses.

He said I'm going to shit into your hand. Then came solvents unto the land and whitened it and the page could become stippled with an arrangement of residues like sea shades and sky shades, umbrellas in Gaza, like the birthmarks of ladies in Proust.

The water needs a forder. Otherwise there's no cutting through to something other. Other than the water. This could not brazen the sea to hold it hard, but the cords that attach us to something could, making this a kind of bath, a voluntary dousing, and not a liquid urging that is animal. We have to decide on our forsakenness to become smooth and hard as a rock that drops, that drops into the dark.

A welder needs the weather. A welder needs the weather so that the white flame of his decision can occur within a climate, and so that the omniscience of this occurrence can incise itself upon the dark surface of distant space, where the truth of all light ravels within its own seeming deconstruction to find it has been eventually inscribed. Burnt but whole on the netherside of a volute without sides, a volute made of dark, which is an annal.

Its folds ask for a hand. The cool rail too beckons. A palm is a surface of transmission, a screen. A palm is a writ surface, which is only evidence, red as a hand. A palm does more than hold fast. A palm goes in and discloses bright jellies like the discharge of tomes. It is made to go in. A palm proves. A palm pales in comparison to all that rushes to surround it. That is its way, and the clement air doesn't mind being cut by it, for a palm is an organ of shooing. There's the alteration; it's made of pain. Its installation was against everybody's will, but they are all dead now, and the fashions have changed.

A clean text is hard against the tongue, like toast well done, which is one way of accepting the doom of morning. A clot of residuals banks up in the mouth; this will have to be gotten rid of somehow. In time, a little softening. Not to bend away from a less delectable air but to find what hardens in it, or how it marks its very going as though a gong. A gong, that is, the grandeur and catastrophe of itself, itself which could be only this single peal and the hundred veilleities of its reverberations, but which can and will be more peals, each one an awful singular, a solid shiverer.

ATE SHAFT TO HILT
TRYING TO BE BORING
MAKING MORE OF IT THAN SHOULD BECAUSE

Wanted too bad to be beyond feeling
In sensation only
And then everything dissolved

It is their arrowroot, their curds
Too that we've borrowed. We did
Not deceive you in the green, we told

You. That, after all, is also theirs. Groomed for fleet
Lands, the quickening of a grass's
Way of flicking shadows around-- theirs.

And: why hair has everything to do with
Love. One of them might have been here, but the point is
Forevermore the phrase he hid, which he might have held up

To foxglove once upon a time. Hid
Inside a minute trembling
Like a dying berry, a drop of sea

Carried out into some enclosure
Where it, the phrase, could shudder
Correctly, that is, with *meaning*. The indiscreet

Line has lost all sense of itself. I am sorry
For it. This is something leftover from the former
Minute. It has a distinct odor.

A sense for language. Cuz a substance with solidity that occurs and is happening. Which does not tell on one like a snitch but perhaps tells in the way years tell on a face. Occurs in one as something always occurring, or taking place like the Aleph of Borges. Imbrecation of memories of others inside of phonemes, excruciating sensitivity. Fishes far away having to do with the shifting ocean floor. A secretion that is happening inside //jackals//bluebells//corny copses fucked the jute// which is beyond subconscious or unconscious, which is subcutaneous, the residue of what a body is doing but somehow in the iterative efflux of sound in which meaning resonates containing also the residue of others who are dead, so that the substance of signification is also ghosts. Something going on in me, because I can feel the substance inside me.

Ander said, I am putting things together, said
I am here for you to be another waiter
Upon the weather, another brother
Of what tugs at vast until

Ander said, I am only wetter than the least
Moist part of water and of the rest I am either equal
Or ether. Either you and I must go together
Or I will draw all things around the absence you leave behind

I am dill, Ander said, upon the salted
Haunch you're roasting, or your glass
Of something out of which today spurts.
I am your own Ander

Ander said, to hoop up what
Could purl toward the murk of your own beginning
To till, or the grouting that has caught everything
All else would have forsaken or forgot

Ander doesn't pluck and is no thorn, is
The ethereal lubricant of bondsmen and churros
And nightshifts who do not know one another yet
But wish, in some recess of their secret density

They knew something other, wholly other,
Of themselves from heavy dose of things that are not them,
Potent because remoter
Than they could have ever dreamt

But it is not the things that do this recognizing
And they do not dream, but emanate a
Part of ourselves that could not harden
Or decline into a thing while still a part of us

A part that erupted out of perforations
We are always making more of, to feel the breeze
Shudder through us where the removèd thing has left behind a chance
For Ander and us to become closer, still, and closer.

A mulch of Emergen-C or her thesis on pornography .
Not being stuffy or even selling the dried-up cigarette
Papers of another age, whose own dust too now has its vintage
But Ander is oddly alone between us, as though in closing

The terrible distances her fund of attributes
Expires, having missed the deadline yet again,
And the vacancy heaves and withdraws
And leaves inside of everything something permanently failed to be achieved

Or even guessed at. The other way of thinking
Is all that is is what is here. But Ander and I know
Your word against mine is not a squaw putting
Twigs in her pan of water, is not the concentration

Of cruelly intelligent, even declarative, natural disasters.
On what is real or not a dwelling can't be built
Can you eat and live on a single feeling or snug and healthful evening,
Can it make up for the bad smell of the man you love

Which will still promise to take hold of you
When you let an afternoon crack
Open and shed its fullness all over you, molten
As pollen on the livid air

When you turn toward the wall again
In the normal anxiety of several hot
Words dropping with enviable precision
Their poison upon the very incomplete

Buffer your lonely body is?

Are you so intelligent your body doesn't have you in it.
Everything could be beautiful maybe.
If it wasn't already a factory.
A milking machine is a machine attached to the valve of a body that is living.
That body has veins and is a little rosy at the teat.
Sucking is the main thing. It is the first thing to be done.
What came first, the milk or the suck.
Whatever she is so full of it.
What came first, the milk or the suck.
She is full of it, full of it, full of it.

The beautiful tension withholding one meaning from another one has blown away

Now there is the beautiful bath of signification, everything swollen and sore with being so much itself

A conjunction inside of which the dream is connected to a sock lidded like your mouth

How any body if Rick or Norbert is to have it you are

To have the melancholy too. Step

Down to cooking up a past you could have been

Loving for longer. How, how light the phalanges of her!

A moth in the smithy of the sun. Not more. Woe.

O woe. Oy vey. I am going to be the figure for tonight. You

Are going to be the cutter of airs the fissures of which I will have

To align myself against. Her tumbled hair had the moonlight.

And piebald and fine designations whose premises you keep on breaking.

We had a promenade happening. I would see a morel.

I saw hurt the mica she was going to be eating me not anymore seeing her.

As usual the lovers forsook her.

Inside of the door is the old theme. I have trouble sitting down..

On the tape I hear a semaphore. Her secret long.

I find a white bone inside of the meat.

I find a white bone inside of the meat.

I find a white bone inside of the meat.

A dowel connects us to the devil's prim lemon.

Fucked him hot in the grits. A butter patting the cordon

At the end of forms, keeping them intact, too intelligent to speak.

Some of them make a death sound.

Some of them small as minnows.

A transmission device smoothes the smoke upon which it founders.

We need to go out for milk. We need to go out for milk.
So?

See how I wow her.
I wow her by putting my ear to her.
See how I wow her. I put my ear to her.

I make all her favors clatter to earth. I make all her favors clatter to earth.
See how I wow her. I put my ear to her. A cloud of forms were there in
the gutter. I think there was a wound in the air. These notes have been
cleansed of all content. These notes have been purified. A frisson! A
sprig of meaning. A garnish! So she had more spit to love. Her item
wanted a fuck. Abstractions upbraid the factual air. Welts swelling on the
backs of things. Welts swelling on the backs of things. In the very heat of
the glove. And sevens. Eights and thens. One time a brace of days fed
her. A broth of nights in her steeping. A broth of nights in her steeping.
Gauze nights wouldn't be good enough. I have the foxglove happening.

This is how sentences first come into the world. And some veins are more equal to her. And the foggy celebrant her chamoix and a wisp of hair. I soberer pegging her wound.

One time I got sick and vomited.

The woman said in the war if you vomited you didn't vomit you had to eat. The woman said in the war if you ever got to put something in you kept it there. You were grateful to have anything.

You didn't reject an offer. One time when I got sick and vomited there was a woman from the war who had been hungry. She knew what food was. The woman said eat it up. The woman said eat up what you have regurgitated.

Eat it. Eat it. Eat it. Eat it. So I. Uh. I ate up the fluids. I began to eat up the burning fluids. There was an I inside of the mistake that was I.

The bile mixed with blood and salt water. I ate it all, I ate up all of it. I ate the air that surrounded it. I ate me out. The sickness was because of me. I ate myself out. I ate myself out.

An asshole with a mouth. A knot that goes on forever but that is not ample. That is tight, impregnable, everywhere. I licked my own pussy. I ate my own shit. I lapped up my vomit. I became self-contained. I didn't need anybody. I didn't need anybody ever again. I loved me. I loved myself. I was self-sufficient. I fucked myself. I was independent. A thing needing no thing. A crewelwork thing locking long on her who wore me. I fit inside myself. I did not exceed myself. The world ricocheted off me. I was finished.

By writing you have to try to get across. There was something about networking. Dirk Bogarde on a side note the hippie bar is Dirk. She was going to empty herself and this was going to take forever.

It still matters what a girl sounds like when she is not trying to make you love her anymore

She bent down with the voles. It was the merry green land happening. A girl is after all what she's got. I don't know. Albumen. I don't know. Albumen. The necktie on him makes me say all the boys in school can't come out to play because it's raining. I don't know why I do a thing. The books in a flower garden because I was always a weak person. Somebody says the soldiers are the bedrock of America. I want to be a bedrock. Therefore I will go to war because nobody touches my body today except her kiss tastes like vegan lasagna. I have a diamond like a runt between my legs. Everyone is glad to see you, your lilywhite hands, the upper room where I balled up the caftan and shoved it in his ass. We went to war because nobody touches my body so I am going to be dead now.

I want this book to be alive because in my life I am dead.

I don't want to become a robot so they will love me as a woman. I am going to Argentina to get fucked. The exquisite sentiments that are ruining me GO GO must die.

Cranked another song out of fiberglass tubing. The sea dromedaries and whether or not children dream of Araby and horses for beauty but everything is a gracious hospitality we don't believe in the hate word is inhospitable to her broad shanks. I won't read this aloud because the intelligent boys will try to hurt me with it.

Real starvation is for poets who don't exist like me.

UNDO ME don't leave me alone. The dismantlement of all fragility. Real starvation is for poets.

Everybody in America is going to die of cancer unless we can die young of passion GO GO.

Lilliputians tie me down and lick me with their little tongues.

Wombs herald the words of their forebears. Have no baby. Where does war go to.

I don't want to hear about your self esteem. My project is CHICK LIT I empty myself so as to become more beautiful I will wear high heels every day in the gutter ruin my legs spreadem any man you meet secretly wants to groom you and/or shit on your face both.

As real as communicativity which language exists to be borrowed a black widow hardened plus broken wings on the window this is

When I die I will become everything A TURDUCKEN

We enter the beautiful dark vision I want to seem like I don't care about myself but only aristocrats can do that I am a peasant I am a hungry.

All this I AM is bad writing. I get off the gurney and hide in the electrical closet all day. The orderly calls me sister the nurse calls me dude. Who the fuck are they. I have to talk to them I don't want to talk.

It's the same old story and you have to learn to speak the CLAMATO language of the elders or they will fuck you too.

You have to learn to speak the deciduous vocables of the true poets a beautiful whiteness.

The feet of white girls in flipflops. Fake hippie skirts from Forever 21. I hate the fop in me I want to eat a nipple of Venus because I am becoming a magnificent woman. Hurting culture want to bleed faggot

Leg wax high heel lipstick cuntface a marketing job designers wanting the best I want filthier but not to be homeless because I love myself too much bluebell cups in the rain a poetics of the music of the poolside therapy. Hate me. We are still thinking too much.

At this site, at this juncture, we are going to be we are becoming free.

Pussy jerky dry. HOLOCAUST FLUFF she says. You don't write that kind of stuff.

When my mother bleeds she likes to have a steak. I like steak. I like the taste. I like it very rare. I like a rare steak with salt and pepper. I like it lean, I like it red. My mother has red hair, red-orange, and she wears lipstick, orange-red. I have her wide feet; they redden when we wear high heels, which we do, because we are small women, and because a small woman in heels gets further than a small woman alone. I know. When I was little and did not want to eat what was on my plate, they told me that if a horse fell down in the ghetto people ran out of their apartments with knives. Hunger. What does one thing have to do with another.

I like the sight of my own blood. It makes me feel alive. I like a blood drive, and to feel the tube warming up with blood; to watch it fill the plastic pouch. Health. A packet of my inestimable substance. I think about what cannot be contained in this world. A box of night? Compounds: Human. Boxcar.

There is a stupidity in the conflation I am in the act of, cow with cattle car and mother with me, cunt and carcass and book and stomach. But this stupidity, if it belongs to me, is also exterior to me. Humans got brutalized by being packed into cattle cars and dying in them or by them which in turn humanizes, necessarily, the suffering of the beasts for which cattle cars were made. Then what. Signification is incestuous, iterative, autofellating. I am not sure this is living. I am not so sure that there is any.

Last year I found myself in Switzerland kind of unexpectedly. I was there for school. I didn't have any money but a Stafford Loan came through just in time. In Switzerland they have banks, cuckoo clocks, mountains, and cows. I was studying in a little tourist town high in the Alps. For a week I couldn't sleep. I listened to Jane Eaglen sing Wagner on my iTunes and looked at the hard Matterhorn and the permafrost, which they say is melting, in strange blue light. I had the shits. All of us did. So much yogurt, so much cream. In class, all you could hear was the professor's voice and the gurgling digestive systems of twenty-odd people. It was hard for us Americans to assimilate so much unctuous dairy product. In Switzerland, they have little vacuum-sealed pots of cream, like the cups of creamer you get with diner coffee in the States. Last year in Switzerland all the little pots of cream had trains on them. This year it was flowers, whatever. But last year.

Different colored train cars, and some cabooses.

I remarked upon them to a few of my professors. Using the local vernacular, I suggested that this conjunction or superimposition of the locomotive and the lactate suggested that technology always already bears the mark of the maternal. Or vice-versa. That transportation has become the womb of the world, the mother of us all. Like in Proust. A modernist idea. Glaucous ova of thinking. Whatever. Everybody was like, yeah.

What suckles, what fuels, what lulls you to sleep. GO. GO.

If the style is too much of an achievement then the edifice becomes what it is, alone, marooned inside of the real. You have to fuck with everything.

Medicated lines. No but the ducts and tubes need your health and have to get rearranged because you were already unnatural. LOVE. Beckett is so complete he is a joke. Stay GO holey or

INCORPORATE. A nice person. Aren't you. How badly do you need the book to estrange itself from "life" so that you can stand it, or how badly does a narrative long to be beautiful. What does poesy care. Some flotsam on top of the lives of nice people. I see only the particulars, and, of these, only the particulars that concern or serve me. I want to live in a world in which it is possible for me to be LOVED WAKE UP and in which I do not hate myself for existing. I want to live in a world in which everybody I know is not on pills because of their feelings POEM GET UP but I know what it is to want to die. I have got to have the smell of semen on my skin GET UP GET UP POEM and not to be afraid of everything easy like feeling and be able to keep on dying going on and capable of FEEL UP UP UP UP

Her belly sawed open and steaming, and stupid waving legs even though her neck GET UP ends in a hole. The steaming world, the annals' restitution, our pleasure as a ball. I actually want to be a woman even though I am supposed to be one.

They have a melancholy aspect, the translators. Even in health. I think that the "long relaxed curve of time" of which John GET UP Ashbery has written could have something to do with the gradualness of the way in which their spines decline and then rise a bit to meet their haunches. Imagine them stacked each upon each like bells in a carillon. Imagine that the word that sounded itself in what rang on the holy day was GOAD, GOAD.

Even I can figure that a body is in a way ultimately an INCENSE. Likewise, pornography has no smell, i.e., NO BODY. The day after I cut garlic my hand smells. The day after I hold a cock I smell it. Many happy returns. Transmission device: the hand. I am not a book UP UP UP

Everything can be put to use except the low. The utterance.

The language of meat doesn't change much. But still if there is something I can do to shit reality by writing I have to.

Wet mall. White white milk wetted my face, fists of it glob around in the air and nothing happens.

There has to be a way to think inside of a wet part or wound me better so that I can feel reality not sucking. Linguals foisted on me by yesterday. Wade through the pyre. I love to be alive.

What if when I put fuckface in the animal I lose sight of the world. Where does meaning end. I have to find out how writing has to do with what happens. I have to find out what happens and how that has to do with time. Only the succor of the beautiful. Only the succor of transmutation.

You just repeal the theatrical aspect of having a life inside of which you are supposed to appear. You just stop showing up. Then you find out that the gift of a body alone doesn't guarantee any kind of life. You abdicate from all violence and you exist. Drug helps. You exist. Your eyes become sticky and swollen; this is from one medicine. Your lips are dry. This is another medicine. The food tastes like nothing and you have the shits or you can't shit. The men around you are not your demographic and the staff doesn't know how to handle you. You do not know what you are and you want to make it easier on them so you figure you might as well be them. You try at least to cultivate a language of dependency but you also keep on saying you don't want the pills. You put yourself to sleep naturally. The natural.

Hymns can make your forgetting happen.
A nightcap I need to put a plaster cast over the moon.
Because this is immediate the after precedes the before.
I need to become the onion stewing in your lap.

I need to become the omen in my own boots, I wish I was a man
I said; he said I wish I was a wish.
A lamp lights the last of us. What's the matter with us.
Well there were too many birds in the scene. They burdened it with
meaning.

Staples well a clitoris it was becoming a beautiful mushroom.
Every valance betokening her, her and her needs, setting up the happy
    lands
With skies ruched and irridescent like old-time Trapper Keepers
The mouth's the haven for all an eye cannot disperse.

Light poured out of the body when we opened it.

An older woman.

Maybe writing is too slow, she said.

The probables are foundering in her, right here. This is the place, she said.

Maybe thought's vestigial.

She stayed gaunt in her intellection; proper.

What did I do.

A curlew, a number.

Pressed in on me.

Troops become the patina.

This is the fundament of authority, she said.

The word that is released trawls something.

A hillock with them on it.

A vantage.

All of us suffering, where did we go.

Put into an animal for safekeeping.

Had to live on something.

Her booty scented. Groomed, hurt.

A life jacket.

A night so thick a suet. Rub sand into its lips
Because I've got to feel it. The speaker is going to become
Alive. Darning the event.
She said

I looked up and was assuaged.
I carried to my mouth the ointment of the cloud that had ceased to move,
That had ceased to pass over me.
I found a secret duct amid these floes of air and then they left off their
coquetries, their complications.
The beauty makes me feel it really happened
The sky had stars in it they glittered like calories upon the world
Energy of the night I upbraided innards that were mine own
In order to become you

Does a resemblance really mean anything.

The world rhymes too much. Maybe.

A situation of the similar kept aloft by an air that is hating.

I spell it like that because I mean it.

Well, maybe a situation can find a way to be a family against your will.

Or maybe that's just psychoanalysis, I was going to write.

All this "meaning." It is rhyme. Is just rhyme.

And this, this could be it. Liberty.

I am harassed.

Tonight three guys in a car said can we help you with your hardon.

That was the most genderfuck catcall I ever pretended I wasn't hearing as I walked by it.

I am so tired, deep deep inside. I am tired.

This ceaseless squabble. What Mandelstam said.

What. Now what. Go on. Go on.

This book contains text from many sources, including JOHN ASHBERY, *SELF-PORTRAIT IN A CONVEX MIRROR;* AUVERMANN, KALBASI, AND AHMED, *CARCASS DISPOSAL: A COMPREHENSIVE REVIEW;* CHARLES BAUDELAIRE, *OEUVRES COMPLÈTES;* THE BIBLE, KING JAMES EDITION; WILLIAM BURROUGHS, *THE SOFT MACHINE;* PAUL CELAN, *THE POEMS OF PAUL CELAN* (TRANS. MICHAEL HAMBURGER); HÉLÈNE CIXOUS, *STIGMATA;* ALEISTER CROWLEY: *MAGICK WITHOUT TEARS;* DELEUZE & GUATTARI, *A THOUSAND PLATEAUS;* MARGUERITE DURAS, *ÉCRIRE;* THE KORAN (TRANS M.H. SHAKIR); *THE MERCK VETERINARY MANUAL;* MARCEL PROUST: *À LA RECHERCHE DU TEMPS PERDU;* RAINER MARIA RILKE, *DUINO ELEGIES* (TRANS. LEISHMAN & SPENDER); GERTRUDE STEIN, *TENDER BUTTONS, HOW TO WRITE;* www.wr2.net/index.html,

Fence Books has a mission to redefine the terms of accessibility by publishing challenging writing distinguished by idiosyncrasy and intelligence rather than by allegiance with camps, schools, or cliques. It is part of our mission to support writers who might otherwise have difficulty being recognized because their work doesn't answer to either the mainstream or to recognizable modes of experimentation.

The Motherwell Prize is an annual series that offers publication of a first or second book of poems by a woman, as well as a five thousand dollar cash prize.

The Fence Modern Poets Series is open to manuscripts by poets of any gender and at any stage of career, and offers a one thousand dollar cash prize in addition to publication.

Fence Books is also a participating publisher in the National Poetry Series.

For more information about these prizes, or about *Fence*, visit www.fenceportal.org.

FENCE BOOKS

THE MOTHERWELL PRIZE

Negro League Baseball	Harmony Holiday
living must bury	Josie Sigler
Aim Straight at the Fountain and Press Vaporize	Elizabeth Marie Young
Unspoiled Air	Kaisa Ullsvik Miller

THE ALBERTA PRIZE

The Cow	Ariana Reines
Practice, Restraint	Laura Sims
A Magic Book	Sasha Steensen
Sky Girl	Rosemary Griggs
The Real Moon of Poetry and Other Poems	Tina Brown
Celona	
Zirconia	Chelsey Minnis

FENCE MODERN POETS SERIES

The Other Poems	Paul Legault
Nick Demske	Nick Demske
Duties of an English Foreign Secretary	Macgregor Card
Star in the Eye	James Shea
Structure of the Embryonic Rat Brain	Christopher Janke
The Stupefying Flashbulbs	Daniel Brenner
Povel	Geraldine Kim
The Opening Question	Prageeta Sharma
Apprehend	Elizabeth Robinson
The Red Bird	Joyelle McSweeney

NATIONAL POETRY SERIES

A Map Predetermined and Chance	Laura Wetherington
	selected by C. S. Giscombe
The Network	Jena Osman
	selected by Prageeta Sharma
The Black Automaton	Douglas Kearney
	selected by Catherine Wagner
Collapsible Poetics Theater	Rodrigo Toscano
	selected by Marjorie Welish